# KENYA
## in Pictures

Catherine Broberg

Lerner Publications Company

# Contents

Lerner Publications Company
A division of Lerner Publishing Group
241 First Avenue North
Minneapolis, MN 55401 U.S.A.

Website address: www.lernerbooks.com

web enhanced @ www.vgsbooks.com

## Cultural Life
48

► Customs. Urban and Rural Life. Religion. Sports and Recreation. Literature. Music. Food.

## The Economy
58

► Agriculture. Manufacturing. Tourism. Transportation. The Future.

## For More Information

Library of Congress Cataloging-in-Publication Data

Broberg, Catherine.
      Kenya in pictures / by Catherine Broberg—Rev. and expanded.
         p.   cm. — (Visual geography series)
      Rev. ed. of: Kenya in pictures / prepared by Geography Department.
      Includes bibliographical references and index.
      Summary: A brief overview of Kenya's land, history, government, people, and culture.
      ISBN: 0-8225-1957-7 (lib. bdg. : alk. paper)
      1. Kenya. 2. Kenya—Pictorial works. [1. Kenya.] I. Kenya in pictures. II. Title. III. Visual geography
series (Minneapolis, Minn.)
DT433.522 .B76 2003
916.762—dc21                                                                   2001003829

Manufactured in the United States of America
1 2 3 4 5 6 - JR - 08 07 06 05 04 03

# INTRODUCTION

The Republic of Kenya—a country of immense natural beauty, wildlife, and diversity—was once viewed as an African success story. It had made a relatively smooth transition from its colonial history to full independence. In recent years, however, Kenya has encountered numerous economic, political, and health-related challenges. If the young nation is to succeed in the twenty-first century, its people must find a way to live up to the national motto—*harambee*, which is Swahili for "pull together."

Kenyans have pulled together in the past. After achieving independence from Great Britain on December 12, 1963, and becoming Africa's thirty-fourth independent nation, Kenyans rejoiced at the conclusion of sixty-eight years of colonial rule. The country, made up of about thirty diverse ethnic groups, then entered a period of relative stability. Although it faced many problems, Kenya avoided major ethnic conflicts and maintained a reasonably efficient administrative system. Living standards, education, health, housing, and economic

activity all improved, and the nation became a respected voice in the United Nations as well as in the African community.

The 1990s and early 2000s, however, were a turbulent time for the East African nation. During this period, Kenya experienced episodes of ethnic violence, which resulted in thousands of deaths, lowered the morale of Kenyans, and frightened away tourists. Political divisions and corruption were other marks of this era, as numerous political parties formed and attempted to challenge the administration of President Daniel T. arap Moi, whose fifth term in office expires in early 2003. Some experts speculate that Moi will attempt to retain power, even though the constitution forbids him to run for another term. Whether Moi or a new party comes out on top in the next election, Kenya is at a critical juncture in its political history.

In addition to political stress, Kenya has suffered from recurring drought, which in turn has affected the country's food supply, its economic stability, and the well-being of its inhabitants.

The health of Kenyan citizens has also been severely endangered by the epidemic of AIDS (acquired immunodeficiency syndrome), which is having a deadly impact throughout the African continent.

Yet the country is not without its share of advantages. Kenya enjoys a wealth of natural and human resources that often bring international recognition. For example, the world turns its attention to this African country in the sports arena, where elite track and field athletes win title upon title. Kenya is also renowned for its abundant wildlife that once delighted big-game hunters and in modern times thrills tourists and other animal observers. Kenya provides an example of cooperation, as its diverse population, for the most part, has found a way to live together in harmony. Drawing on and protecting these strengths will be more important than ever for Kenya as it faces the challenges of the twenty-first century.

Olympic gold and silver medals in the 3000-meter steeplechase await **Kenyan athletes** Reuben Kosgei Seroney (front) and Wilson Boit Kipketer (behind Serony) at the 2000 Olympic games in Sydney, Australia.

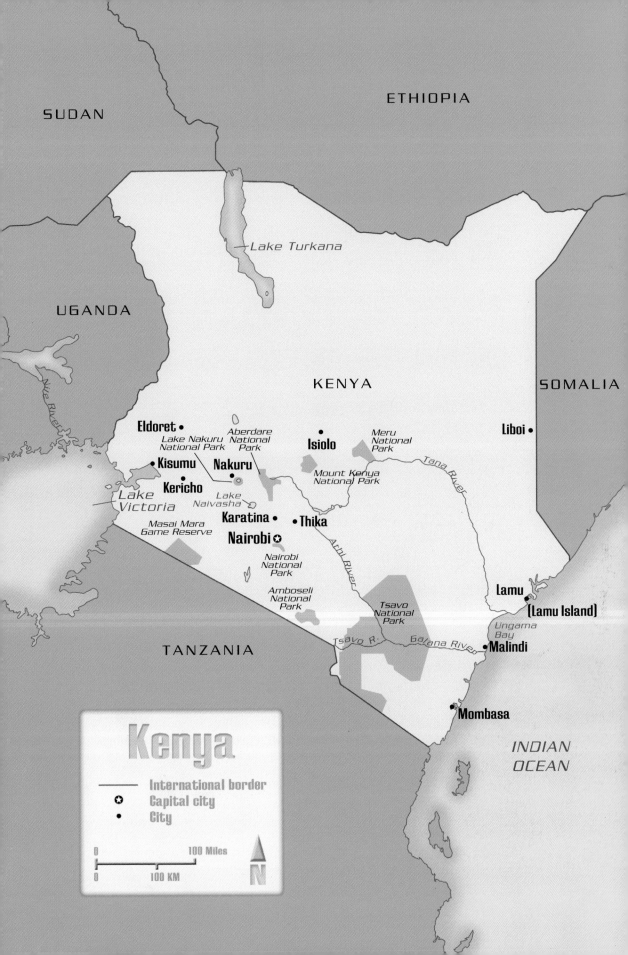

# THE LAND

Kenya, which straddles the equator, is located on the eastern coast of the continent of Africa. Bounded on the southeast by the Indian Ocean, Kenya shares borders with Tanzania to the south, Uganda to the west, Sudan to the northwest, Ethiopia to the north, and Somalia to the northeast. With a total area of 224,960 square miles (582,644 square kilometers), Kenya is slightly smaller than the state of Texas.

Most of the land—roughly the northern three-fifths of the country—is desertlike and unable to sustain a large population. In contrast, the southern two-fifths of Kenya has a mild climate and receives plentiful rainfall. Home to 85 percent of Kenya's people, this area also generates nearly all the economic activity in the country.

## ○ Topography

Kenya has four distinct geographical regions. One region, the southeastern coast, fronts on the Indian Ocean at sea level. Moving inland and northward, the land gradually rises in elevation to the capital city

of Nairobi, approximately 300 miles (483 km) from the coast. A second region encompasses the land surrounding Nairobi and reaches a plateau averaging nearly 5,000 feet (1,524 meters) in height. A third area is the arid northern region above the equator, which ranges from 500 feet (152 m) above sea level on its eastern side to 5,000 feet (1,524 m) on its western side.

Kenya's fourth topographical region, which lies in the southwest, comprises a highland plateau broken up by two mountain ranges—the Aberdare Range and the Mau Escarpment. These two mountain ranges run north to south through west central Kenya and average 10,000 to 11,000 feet (3,048 to 3,353 m) in elevation. Running between the Aberdares and the Mau Escarpment, the Rift Valley separates the cliffs formed by the two ranges.

The Rift Valley in Kenya is part of the Great Rift Valley. This vast depression of land begins in southwestern Asia and cuts its way across the African continent through Kenya's western highlands and south to

**Lake Victoria** became known to Europeans in 1858, when John Hanning Speke was searching for the source of the Nile River. Speke named the lake to honor Britain's Queen Victoria. Up until this time, the lake had been known to local peoples as Ukerewe.

Mozambique. Formed by volcanic action, the Great Rift Valley varies in altitude. Within Kenya, the valley floor is quite high in elevation, rising to more than 6,000 feet (1,829 m) above sea level at Lake Naivasha.

Located in the center of Kenya just south of the equator, Mount Kenya is the highest peak in the country. With an altitude of 17,058 feet (5,199 m), this extinct volcano is the second highest mountain on the African continent after Mount Kilimanjaro in Tanzania. Another prominent peak, Mount Elgon (14,178 ft; 4,321 m), lies on Kenya's western border with Uganda.

## Rivers and Lakes

Kenya has three water drainage systems—the coastal lowlands, where rivers drain into the Indian Ocean, the Rift Valley system, where streams feed into a chain of lakes within the valley, and a group of small streams to the west of the Rift Valley that flow into Lake Victoria at Kenya's southwestern boundary. The chief rivers flow through the coastal lowlands in south central and southeastern Kenya.

Beginning its 440-mile (708-km) course on the eastern edge of the Rift Valley, the Tana River is the longest river in Kenya. The Tana wanders southward and eastward, becoming navigable about 150 miles (241 km) from Ungama Bay, where it empties into the Indian Ocean. The 340 mile (547 km) long Galana River is formed by the merging of two waterways, the Athi from central Kenya and the Tsavo from southern Kenya near Tanzania. Several miles north of the seaport town of Malindi, the Galana River empties into the Indian Ocean.

## AFRICA'S GREAT LAKE

Lake Victoria is the second largest lake in the world (only North America's Lake Superior is larger in area). Lake Victoria is about 250 miles (402 km) long and 200 miles (322 km) wide. At its deepest point, it is 265 feet (81 m) deep. Kenya, Uganda, and Tanzania all border the lake.

Lake Victoria is also the main source of Africa's Nile River, which bisects Uganda and winds northward through Sudan and Egypt on its way to the Mediterranean Sea.

Owen Falls Dam at Lake Victoria created the world's largest hydroelectric reservoir upon completion in 1954. While newer facilities generate more power, Lake Victoria remains the largest storage reservoir in the world, holding 7.2 billion cubic feet (204 million cubic meters) of water.

In addition to rivers, several lakes water Kenya. Two of Africa's great lakes—Victoria and Turkana—cross Kenya's borders. Gigantic Lake Victoria, part of which lies in Kenya's southwestern corner, is the world's second largest freshwater body. Only North America's Lake Superior is bigger. Lake Turkana lies almost entirely within northern Kenya, except for a small part of its northern shore, which pushes into Ethiopia.

Five bodies of water make up a chain of lesser lakes on the floor of the Rift Valley. About 40 miles (64 km) northwest of Nairobi lies Lake Naivasha, the largest in the chain—a beautiful lake with striking, clear blue waters.

## ◉ Climate

Although Kenya straddles the equator, high altitudes in the central and western portions of the country temper the climate. Along the coast, the temperature averages 69°F (21°C) to 90°F (32°C) year-round. Near Nairobi the average ranges from 45°F (7°C) to 80°F (27°C), depending on the time of day. Significant temperature changes occur between afternoon and evening, but the climate varies more in terms of rainfall than temperature.

Kenya is mainly an agricultural nation, so its rains are of utmost importance to the economy. Kenya has two rainy seasons separated by two dry periods. The two rainy seasons are the long rains from April to June and the short rains from October to December. During the remaining months of the year, Kenya is dry but may have occasional shower activity. January, February, August, and September are the driest months.

The rainy seasons occur regularly each year and, while they last, rain falls from one to four hours daily. The northern regions above the equator hardly receive any rain at all, but the coastal, central, and western parts of the country receive more than 40 inches (102 centimeters) of rain each year.

The 1990s and early 2000s were times of severe drought interrupted by floods in 1997–1998 related to the El Niño and La Niña climate changes (disruptions of ocean atmosphere systems in the tropical Pacific that affect weather around the globe). In late 2000, experts believed that 3.3 million Kenyans were suffering from an East African drought that affected northern and eastern Kenya in particular. The drought led to crop failure, livestock decline and death, and, consequently, food shortages for the region. International aid organizations were working to prevent widespread famine by distributing food to the affected areas and by helping farmers prepare for the next growing season.

## ▶ Flora

Thousands of flowers—both wild and cultivated—grow in the southern two-thirds of Kenya. Plant life on the coast is tropical, diverse, and lush. Coconut palms and dense mangrove forests, as well as teak and sandalwood trees, fringe the coast of the Indian Ocean. Inland, the coastal vegetation thins out to thorny scrub, along with occasional acacia (flowering thorn trees) and baobab (broad-trunked trees with edible fruit). This zone of scrubby vegetation broadens as it merges with the semidesert region bordering Somalia to the northeast.

At interior elevations of 3,000 feet (914 m) or more, broad grasslands cover the land, and acacia groves line the riverbanks. Areas receiving the most rainfall often sprout groves of giant bamboo. In the south central highlands around Nairobi, some flowering trees can be found. Among them is the jacaranda, a tall tree that has showy purple blue blossoms in the springtime. Flowers and shrubs in this region grow in a splendid range of sizes, shapes, and colors. Bougainvillea, for example—with its many-shaded blossoms of purple, red, orange, or white—can grow to be 16 feet (5 m) high.

To the west, at higher altitudes, impressive giant lobelias and groundsels are common. Dense forests of pines and deciduous trees (which shed their leaves each year) appear as the land rises above 6,000 feet (1,829 m). In early 2001, experts advised Kenya to stop its program of deforestation. They cautioned that plans to clear areas for housing near Mount Kenya and elsewhere would threaten the environment and harm the economy, as forests affect the health of their surroundings and are a source of medicines.

"Forests are the **earth's green lungs**, helping to remove carbon dioxide and other pollutants from the atmosphere. They also stabilise soils, reducing the risks of erosion and runoff into rivers, and are in many cases home to a rich variety of wildlife and indigenous, forest-dwelling peoples. Forests also provide food, shelter and medicines and are a rich source of therapeutic compounds from which companies can derive new, potential cures for diseases from AIDS to cancer."

—Klaus Topfer, United Nations Environment Program Executive Director

Generous rains in Kenya's south central highlands allow many flower species to achieve astonishing sizes. These wild **poinsettias** may grow up to 15 feet (4.5 m) tall.

## Fauna

The wildlife of Kenya is among the most abundant and varied in the world, and several large game parks have been established so that wildlife enthusiasts can observe animals in their natural habitats. Large animals such as elephants, giraffes, buffalo, and rhinoceroses roam the high plains in sizable numbers, as do zebras and several kinds of antelope—impalas, wildebeests, hartebeests, and gazelles. Here, too, are beasts of prey—lions, cheetahs, leopards, hyenas, jackals, and wild dogs. Smaller animals, such as tree hyraxes and monkeys, inhabit both the highland plains and forestlands farther southwest.

On the Kenyan high plains, **giraffes** scan the far horizon for predators. For links to photographs and other information on safaris and African wildlife, go to vgsbooks.com.

Female as well as male **Cape buffalo** grow formidable horns. If attacked, the herd will form a ring around its young, blind, and crippled members. Predators rarely harvest any but the oldest, solitary-living males.

In 1990 Kenya's Wildlife Conservation and Management Department became the Kenya Wildlife Service (KWS) and was charged with protecting and conserving the country's wildlife. One of the first goals for this new conservation service, under the direction of Dr. Richard Leakey, was to end the endemic poaching (illegal hunting) in Kenya that was nearly exterminating the rhinoceros populations and having dire effects on its elephant herds. Kenya's elephant population fell from 140,000 in 1972 to a low of 19,000 at the height of the poaching epidemic of the 1970s and 1980s. In the early 2000s, through conservation efforts, the population had risen to 29,000.

As of the early 2000s, the KWS has made great strides in reducing poaching in Kenya. A 1989 international ban on the import of ivory

## IVORY

**Rhinoceroses and elephants have long been hunted for their ivory horns and tusks. Traditionally ivory has been used for carving figurines or jewelry or for making products such as dice, chess sets, and piano keys. Ivory continues to be a popular art medium, particularly in Japan. A sale of stockpiled ivory to that country in 1997 boosted poaching in Kenya, just as its rhinoceros population was begining to recover from the decimation of previous decades.**

helped in these efforts by drastically decreasing the ivory market. In 1997 three southern African nations (Zimbabwe, Namibia, and Botswana) were allowed to sell stockpiles of ivory to Japan. Some experts argue that this sale has again led to a slight poaching increase in Kenya.

Birds common to Kenya's highlands include ostriches, eagles, kites, and vultures. Lakeshores and coastal waters swarm with pelicans, cranes, ibis, storks, egrets, and flamingos. Throughout the southern two-thirds of the country, a variety of brightly colored parakeets, parrots, and songbirds are found.

Many kinds of reptiles, from small salamanders to sizable crocodiles, are plentiful in Kenya. Although some reptiles are large or poisonous, in general they are not aggressive and avoid people. The largest of more than one hundred species of snakes is the gigantic but nonpoisonous python. Many smaller snakes—puff adders, vipers,

The **black rhinoceros** found in Kenya may derive its name from the dark local soil that often coats its skin after a refreshing roll in dust or mud.

mambas, and cobras—are deadly. Insects such as mosquitoes, bees, and flies often carry diseases, which threaten both humans and animals.

The Nile perch and the tilapia thrive in Kenya's lakes and waterways. Trout, which have been introduced into the cool waters of the Aberdare Mountains, offer plenty of good fishing. Kenya's coastal waters are home to large tropical fish— sharks, marlin, sailfish, yellowfin tuna, dorada, and barracuda.

The **marabou** is the largest member of the stork family. The adult marabou can grow up to 5 feet (1.5 m) tall with a wingspan of 8 feet (2.4 m).

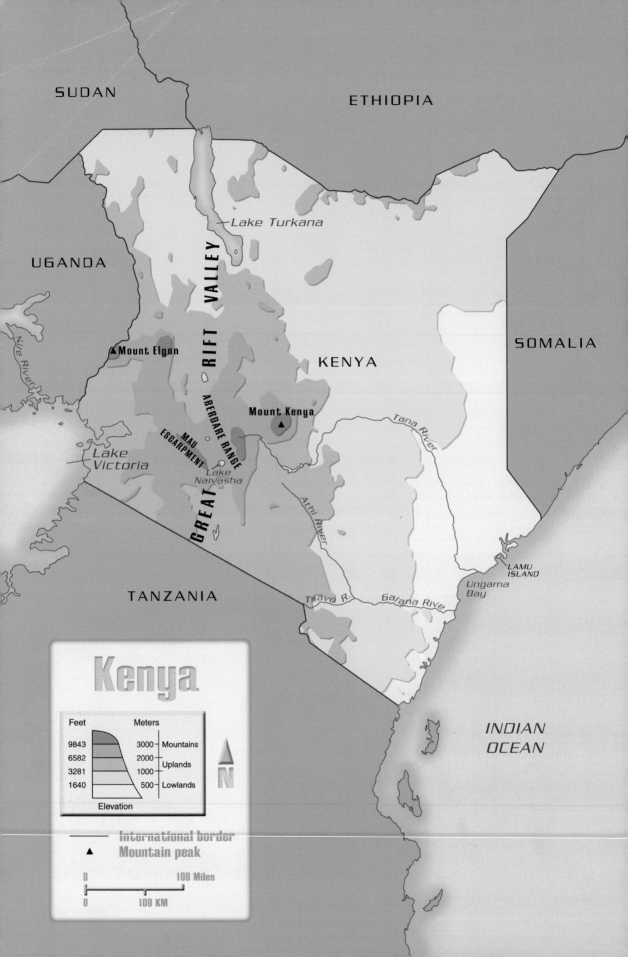

SUDAN

ETHIOPIA

UGANDA

*Lake Turkana*

SOMALIA

KENYA

RIFT VALLEY

▲Mount Elgon

ABERDARE RANGE

MAU ESCARPMENT

Mount Kenya ▲

*Tana River*

*Lake Naivasha*

*Nile River*

Lake Victoria

*Athi River*

GREAT

LAMU ISLAND

*Ungama Bay*

TANZANIA

*Tsavo R.*

*Galana River*

INDIAN OCEAN

## Kenya

| Feet | Meters | |
|------|--------|---|
| 9843 | 3000 | Mountains |
| 6582 | 2000 | Uplands |
| 3281 | 1000 | |
| 1640 | 500 | Lowlands |

Elevation

N

International border
▲ Mountain peak

0        100 Miles

0        100 KM

## Cities

Kenya has a number of important manufacturing towns—Mombasa, Eldoret, Nakuru, and Thika—as well as the chief industrial center and capital city, Nairobi. These urban areas are home to about 33 percent of Kenya's population. Since the 1970s, many Kenyans in search of better jobs and living conditions have been moving from rural areas into large cities. Consequently, Kenya's urban areas are growing so fast that the cities' resources cannot meet the needs of all their residents, and the standard of living in Kenya's cities has declined. In the 1990s, the unemployment rate in urban areas was at about 35 percent. Additionally, new residents did not have access to sufficient numbers of good-quality, low-cost homes.

**NAIROBI** Since its founding in 1899, Nairobi has grown into a metropolis of about two million people. Life in the capital is fast paced, and a visitor would find little difference between living in Nairobi and living in any other urban area. A mixture of cultures, Nairobi is home to Africans, Asians, and Europeans, making it a truly international city.

**Nairobi's** name became official in 1899. The city was built at the watering hole indigenous herders preferred for their cattle. The locals called the spot Enkare Nairobi, which means "place of cold (or sweet) water."

Nairobi is one of Africa's most beautiful and productive cities, rivaling Cairo in Egypt and Johannesburg in South Africa as a busy road, rail, and air hub. National and international organizations based in Nairobi influence events across the entire African continent. Most Kenyan government buildings are located in Nairobi, including those that house the Kenyan legislature and all of the ministries.

SECONDARY CITIES In contrast to Nairobi, Mombasa—Kenya's leading port on the Indian Ocean—is a very old settlement. The first Arab traders probably lived in Mombasa during the eleventh century A.D. Much smaller than Nairobi, Mombasa has a population of 600,000. Perhaps

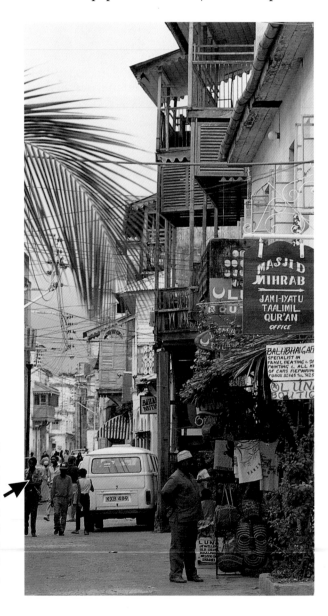

Narrow streets and tall houses with open, airy balconies reflect Mombasa's historical and cultural links with the Arab-Islamic world. Visit vgsbooks.com for links to more information about Kenya's two largest cities, Nairobi and Mombasa.

A **worker on a tea estate** near Kericho harvests tea leaves. Most tea is harvested this way. Available machines cannot distinguish between the high-quality leaves at the tips of branches and the coarser leaves nearest the trunk of the plant.

because of its size and its warm climate, Mombasa has a slower pace of life than does Nairobi. A large Arab population and many buildings modeled on Middle Eastern architecture contribute to an atmosphere in Mombasa that is quite different from any other large city in Kenya. Because of its excellent beaches on the Indian Ocean, Mombasa is also Kenya's chief resort city.

Most of Kenya's cities developed because of their proximity to a trade route or to land suited to a certain crop. For example, Kericho (population 40,000) began as a trading town to serve the large tea-growing estates in the region. People still come to Kericho to work on these estates.

Two other cities that owe their importance to their location are Nakuru (population 163,000) and Kisumu (population 201,000). Founded as a trading post in the heart of the Rift Valley, Nakuru is situated along the Rift Valley between Kenya's western border and Nairobi. Kisumu, on Lake Victoria, became a rail center for products from Mombasa destined for Uganda, northern Tanzania, and the Democratic Republic of Congo. Surrounded by good farmland and fine grazing land, Kisumu became a meeting place for traders of crops and cattle.

# HISTORY AND GOVERNMENT

Archaeologists have uncovered bones and tools of early peoples throughout Kenya, but the majority of the finds have come from the Rift Valley region. Few facts are known about these early humans and their cultures, but their tools and fossil remains have convinced historians that people lived in East Africa as early as two million years ago.

Arabs initiated the first outside contacts with Kenya's inhabitants about two thousand years ago. About five hundred years later, Greeks, Romans, Persians, and East Indians began trading with the people who lived along Kenya's coast. The traders recorded information about the best time of the year and the best route to travel on the Indian Ocean, as well as the best time to put ashore. They also told of the ivory and spices they had obtained from the interior. These foreigners did not venture far into Kenya from the coast of the Indian Ocean. Although these ambitious merchants knew people lived in the interior, they did not attempt to meet them.

## Early History

At nearly the same time as this early trading on the coast of Kenya, large migrations were taking place on the African continent. About two thousand years ago, peoples living along the borders of modern Nigeria and Cameroon began moving eastward and southward from their homelands. Forced out of their own territories, in part by a population increase, these people came to the region of present-day Kenya seeking fertile farmland. The newcomers, who spoke languages that evolved into the widespread Bantu language family, firmly established themselves in Kenya by about A.D. 900.

Immigration of Bantu-speaking peoples into Kenya increased until it reached its peak in the fourteenth and fifteenth centuries. During the four to five centuries of Bantu movement, other groups also were migrating. Nilotic peoples (who had originally lived in the Nile River Valley) came from the regions of present-day Sudan and southern Egypt. Cushitic peoples came from present-day Somalia,

## CRADLE OF MANKIND

East Africa has often been called the "cradle of humankind." In 1911 an extraordinary fossil bed was discovered in the Olduvai Gorge in Tanzania near the Kenyan border. These fossils and, later, bones from the region were eventually linked to prehom-inids (hominids are humans and their ancestors).

A British missionaries' son born in Kenya, Dr. Louis Leakey, his wife, Mary, and their second son, Richard, made important discoveries at several East African sites. Their findings greatly expanded our knowledge of human evolution. To learn more, check out these books: Margaret Poynter, *The Leakeys: Uncovering the Origins of Humankind* (Berkeley Heights, NJ: Enslow Publishers, 1997) and Delta Willis, *The Leakey Family: Leaders in the Search for Human Origins* (New York: Facts on File, 1992), or go to vgsbooks.com.

**Louis and Mary Leakey,** British anthropologists (people who study the origins and development of early humans), began their search for prehistoric tools and bones at various sites in East Africa in the 1950s.

from northern Africa, and from the eastern coast. All of these groups encountered the Bantu-speaking peoples in the course of their travels. Kenya was the crossroads for these movements.

While the Bantu-speaking peoples and other groups pushed into Kenya from the north, another force—the Islamic religion—was becoming influential on the eastern coast of Africa. Traders from southwest Asia introduced the religion of Islam—founded by the prophet Muhammad in the seventh century A.D.—into this region by the late eighth century.

The death of Muhammad in A.D. 632 and the growth of Islam between the seventh and tenth centuries indirectly caused the Arab world to take interest in Kenya. As Islam spread in southwest Asia, quarreling arose between those who followed the teachings of Muhammad and those who did not. Many people left the region, in part because of increased population pressures and wars that erupted on the Arabian Peninsula. Escaping by boat, these people were carried by the monsoons (strong, seasonal winds) across the Indian Ocean to East Africa, where they settled along the Kenyan coast.

By the ninth century, various Islamic groups controlled most of Kenya's coastal area through trade. By the eleventh century, they had established settlements, and by the early fifteenth century their trade routes extended to India and China. With the strength of their efficient trade and new religion, the Arab peoples dominated the coast of present-day Kenya for nearly five hundred years, until a new group of foreigners—the Portuguese—arrived.

## Coastal Influences

The Portuguese began to explore the coasts of Africa in the early fifteenth century in search of gold and spices. In 1498 Vasco da Gama led an expedition around the southern tip of the continent (later named the Cape of Good Hope) and up the eastern coast toward what would become Kenya. Finding the prosperous coastal culture of the Arabs, the Portuguese destroyed many Muslim settlements as they searched for gold and spices and fought to gain control of the area. The Portuguese had won control of the Kenyan coast by the early 1500s and used the area as a trading base for approximately two hundred years.

Because Portugal did not find the commodities it wanted in East Africa, Portuguese interest turned to other regions in the mid-1600s. For about the next 150 years, Arabs governed Kenya's profitable coastal trade from the island of Zanzibar off the southeastern tip of Kenya's coast. Neither the Muslims nor the Portuguese, however, greatly influenced the Bantu-speaking

Vasco da Gama was not the first or the only adventurer in his family. His father Estavão and his brother Paulo were both able sea captains for the Portuguese monarchy. Originally João II, king of Portugal, commissioned Estavão to chart a sea route to India, but Estavão died before the expedition could be outfitted. Vasco took his father's place, and when Vasco set out around the Cape of Good Hope in 1498, his brother Paulo accompanied him.

Built in the sixteenth century, **Fort Jesus** in Mombasa was a Portuguese military and trading hub.

population or other peoples in Kenya's interior. With permission from the sultan of Zanzibar, European missionaries began to explore Kenya's interior in 1850.

## Interior Exploration

Before 1859 European knowledge of East Africa had been limited to the coastal areas. Between 1850 and 1870, the search for new markets, raw materials, and cheap labor led to an interest in the inland areas. Along with the missionary activity in Kenya, several other European intrusions into the region occurred during this period. Motivation for exploration was political as well as economic. Concerned that France and Germany were gaining control of regions in Africa, Great Britain also took an interest in East Africa.

Seeking the sources of the Nile and Niger Rivers, as well as knowledge about the vegetation and wildlife of Africa, the British ventured into the Kenya-Uganda region of East Africa. With financial support from the British government, John Speke and James Grant explored the area around Lake Victoria and the Rift Valley. Their

1858 discovery of the source of the Nile River in what is now Uganda heightened British interest in the Kenya-Uganda area.

Germany was also exploring East Africa during this period. The journeys of two German missionaries—Johann Krapf and Johannes Rebmann—in the mid-nineteenth century resulted in the first European contact with the people of the Mount Kenya region. Both German and British exploration in East Africa continued, which caused competition between the two countries. European historians have called this period of accelerated exploration and territorial acquisition, which began in the 1880s, the "scramble for Africa."

## MISSIONARIES

As the word mission suggests, people who set out for missionary work have a distinct purpose in mind—to educate, to spread a religion, or to offer political guidance. Missionaries try to help people in developing countries get information and learn new skills that may improve their lives. At the same time, introduction of outside ideas can lead to the loss of a country's own traditions and culture. In the early 2000s, about 2,300 missionaries were at work in Kenya.

European missionaries first came to Kenya in the mid-nineteenth century. Christian **missionary work** continues throughout Kenya in modern times. In this photograph, a group meets at a Catholic mission near Lake Turkana.

# ◐ British Control

Very little of the African continent was actually controlled by Europeans before the 1880s. Unlike Portugal, Britain and France secured areas of influence for trade and missionary activity, but they did not establish colonies. Between 1880 and 1900, this situation changed dramatically, and European governments gained control over forty of the forty-six political units into which Africa had been divided.

This division of the continent took place at the Berlin Conference of 1884–1885, which was attended by fourteen countries, including Great Britain, France, Germany, Belgium, Portugal, and the United States. Each nation presented claims to various parts of the African continent, and together they formulated rules for colonization as well as rules for trade. Another goal of the conference was to ensure that the mouths and basins of the Nile and Congo Rivers would be accessible to all and open to trade. Even as the conference was being prepared, Germany was strengthening its position in East Africa by quietly signing treaties with African leaders in the area.

The three-month Berlin Conference has been referred to as Africa's undoing. European powers staked their claims to territories in Africa without negotiating with the African people. Their division of the continent did not follow the existing settlements or the established boundaries of the continent's various ethnic groups. On the contrary, the new maps divided some close-knit ethnic groups and combined others who had little in common or who were even adversaries. As a result, political division and unrest continue to haunt Africa.

East Africa—including what is now Kenya—was divided between the British and the Germans, with the land north of the middle of Lake Victoria claimed by the British and with everything south of this line placed under German control. At first Kenya was largely ignored by the British, who were much more interested in Uganda and the headwaters of the Nile River. Britain feared that if it did not control Uganda, another European power might take over the area and dam up the Nile River at its source.

Once the British were established in Uganda, Kenya became important as Uganda's link to the sea. In 1896 the British Parliament allotted funds for the building of the Kenya-Uganda Railroad, which

Under close British supervision, East Indian laborers cleared the way for the first railroad line across Kenya, which was completed in the early1900s.

would link the historic port of Mombasa with Uganda and the Nile region. Work began in 1896, and, despite numerous hardships, the new railway line reached Nairobi—300 miles (483 km) from Mombasa—in 1899. By 1901 the line stretched approximately 500 miles (805 km) from Mombasa to Lake Victoria. A few years later, it reached Uganda.

The British forcibly transported thousands of East Indians to work on the railway as indentured servants, believing that they would be easier to control than the local African population. Many East Indians remained in Kenya upon the completion of the railway. They opened small stores, became businesspeople, or continued as employees of the railway. They could not become landowners, however, because the British government did not allow nonwhites to purchase land in the British territory—known as the East African Protectorate.

Although occupation of Kenya had not been foremost in the minds of the politicians who recommended the railway, the British government gave and sold choice land in Kenya to European settlers in order to make the railroad profitable. The offer did not attract an impressive number of colonists, but those who did come planted large tracts of land and became quite wealthy.

## Seeds of Conflict

Among the many problems encountered by the East Africa Protectorate were disagreements between the European settlers and the colonial administration. To give the newcomers some responsibility in running the protectorate, the British established the Legislative Council in 1905. By the end of World War I (1914–1918), the nine thousand Europeans in Kenya exercised their representative voice in the government through the Legislative Council.

The black population, however, had no political power in the protectorate. Although the British government officially claimed to be concerned with the rights of blacks, the government allotted the choicest lands to the white minority and forced blacks to relocate on less fertile areas that had been set aside for them. In addition, the Europeans discouraged blacks and Asians from farming for themselves, hiring them instead to work on the large, European-owned estates.

## The Twentieth Century

During World War I, Germany—Britain's enemy in Europe and rival in Africa—raided and harassed the British in East Africa. After the war ended in 1918, the Germans lost their Tanganyika colony (later called Tanzania) south of Kenya, and the British added it to their Kenya-Uganda possessions.

World War I had important effects on Kenya. Many settlers had been called to serve in the British army, and the export economy was hurt by their absence. The white population of Kenya increased after the war, however, as former soldiers were given land to settle in the protectorate. By changing the status and name of the East Africa Protectorate to the Kenya Colony and Protectorate in 1920, Great Britain officially proclaimed Kenya as part of its empire.

During the period between World War I and World War II (1939–1945), significant political forces were at work in Kenya. In the early 1920s, the Asian population raised the issue of representation in the colonial administration. Asians, who far outnumbered white settlers, wanted voting rights and representation on the Legislative Council. Europeans resisted the demand, and the issue was taken to Great Britain. Fearing that violence in the colony would increase financial costs for the military and police, the British government permitted Asians to have representatives on the council, although they had no voting rights.

Between 1929 and 1944, thousands of displaced black Kenyans sought new lives in Nairobi. The city's population tripled from 33,000 to 109,000 in that time period.

## The Rise of Kenyan Nationalism

Perhaps the most important development of the period between the two world wars was the emergence of black Kenyans as a political force. Pushed off their land, many Kenyans, especially those of the Kikuyu ethnic group, took jobs in urban areas such as Nairobi and Nakuru. City life, however, was difficult because of rising taxes, falling wages, and the introduction of black identification passes—which the British colonial administration deemed necessary to control blacks. In response, these workers entered the political arena, becoming Kenya's first nationalistic group.

The political activity of black Kenyans spread in the 1920s and 1930s. The most prominent Kenyan political organization before World War II was the Kikuyu Central Association (KCA), which was formed in 1925. Jomo Kenyatta (then known as Johnston Kamau) became its general secretary in 1928. In 1929 Kenyatta went to Great Britain to petition the British government for elected black representation on the Legislative Council, but the petition was ignored. It was not until 1944 that the first black Kenyan was nominated to the Legislative Council.

In 1946 Jomo Kenyatta—who had been writing and attending a university in Britain since 1931—returned to Kenya and assumed leadership of the newly formed Kenya African Union (KAU). This group put demands for ethnic, economic, and political equality before the British government, but all were refused.

## Midcentury Uprisings

From 1948 to 1950, discontent smoldered among all Kenyans, but particularly among blacks. Since their negotiations with the British government were unsuccessful, black Kenyans formed secret political societies—one of which became known as Mau Mau. Committing acts of violence, some secret societies directed their frustrations toward the colonial government and the Europeans in Kenya. The terrorists' goal

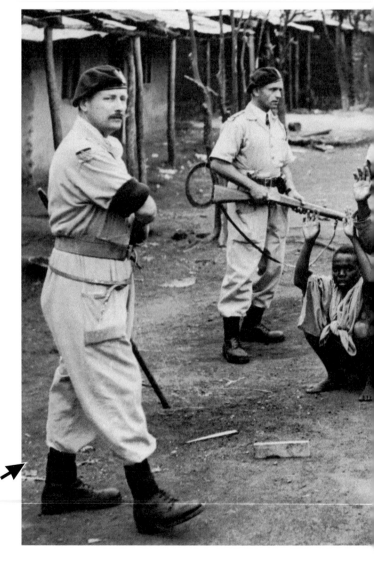

In a village near Nairobi in 1953, **British colonial police** detain suspected agitators. Others search the village for evidence of Mau Mau terrorist activity.

was to keep the colonial government off balance and to prevent whites in Kenya from gaining independence from Britain—that is, independence without equal rights for black Kenyans.

Terrorist activities increased in number and violence, reaching riot proportions. In October 1952, the British colonial governor declared a state of emergency, and all black Kenyan political parties were outlawed in 1953. Lumped together by the British government under the name Mau Mau, the secret societies were believed to be linked to the KAU.

Black Kenyans endured many restrictions during the state of emergency. People fled to the forests to avoid the police. Police rounded up hundreds of black Kenyan political leaders and held hasty trials, after which most of the important political leaders—including Jomo Kenyatta—were imprisoned in 1953. In the meantime, the secret societies attempted to keep the spirit of rebellion alive while their leaders were in jail. Although the state of emergency lasted through 1960, most of the Mau Mau terrorist activity and the resulting British retaliations occurred between 1952 and 1955.

## ◉ The Road to Independence

Beginning in the late 1950s, other ethnic groups joined the Kikuyu to demand black Kenyan rule. In June 1955, the ban on political parties was lifted—excluding the parties of the Kikuyu—and many small, ethnically based parties were formed. The Kenya African National Union (KANU), which was the party most similar to the KAU, became the largest of these. Its main rival party, the Kenya African Democratic Union (KADU), also became quite powerful. The unifying element of these parties was the desire for the release of Jomo Kenyatta. The groups also wanted a general election for black Kenyan representatives to the Legislative Council.

Kenya's first prime minister, **Jomo Kenyatta** *(left)*, discusses an amnesty program for rebels with Mau Mau leader, Mwariama *(right)*.

In the late 1950s, Kenyan politicians also faced the problem of whether to push for independence from Britain as well as for majority (black Kenyan) rule. By 1959 political activism was making it obvious to the British government that Kenyans would settle for nothing less than independence with majority rule. This meant the majority of seats in the legislature would have to be held by black Kenyans because they made up the largest segment of the population. In January 1960, a constitutional conference was held in Britain that established majority rule as the basic principle of the forthcoming Kenyan constitution.

Finally, in February 1961, elections were held to choose black Kenyan representatives for a new parliament (legislative body). The KANU party won the elections, but its representatives refused to take office until Jomo Kenyatta—the acknowledged party leader—was released from prison. The British did not meet this demand until August 1961, and, in the meantime, the rival KADU party formed a government. Nevertheless, Kenyatta's eventual release represented British cooperation in Kenya's independence.

# Building a Nation

Declaring their independence from Great Britain on December 12, 1963, Kenyans elected the KANU party to choose a governmental system for the new nation. Jomo Kenyatta became Kenya's first prime minister. The following year, Kenya became a republic (a sovereign state ruled by elected representatives) with Kenyatta as its president. In the same year, the minority KADU party—which had been formed by several small ethnic groups that feared domination by the large groups of Kikuyu and Luo—joined the KANU party.

Under Kenyatta the government overhauled the colonial economic and cultural systems. It took over farms and businesses that had been held by Europeans who had not become Kenyan citizens, selling or renting these properties to black Kenyans. The government expanded both public and private education. Kenyatta also created a sense of national pride among peoples who historically had more loyalty to their individual ethnic groups than to the national government.

Kenyatta died in 1978 at the age of eighty-six. He had governed Kenya from the time of independence until the time of his death. Vice president Daniel T. arap Moi was Kenyatta's successor and began his presidency by continuing the moderate economic policies begun by Kenyatta. A few powerful Kenyans have come to dominate the nation's politics during arap Moi's has been presidency, however. This situation has encouraged corruption and has aggravated ethnic tensions.

In November of 1978, after serving ninety days as Kenya's acting president, **Daniel T. arap Moi** celebrates his official election to the presidency.

# ◉ Human Rights Issues

After a failed coup (violent overthrow) by members of the Kenya Air Force in 1982, the government cracked down on dissent. Subsequent charges of human rights abuses have strained Kenya's relations with the international community. Donors and lenders—including the International Monetary Fund (IMF) and the World Bank—have repeatedly suspended aid to the nation until economic and political reforms have progressed.

Human rights watchdog groups, such as Amnesty International and Africa Watch, as well as Roman Catholic bishops, have spoken out against a variety of issues in Kenya, including the treatment of political prisoners in Kenya, the practice of female circumcision among some sectors of the population, the unfairness of Kenyan trials, and the government's power over the judicial system. The government has also been condemned for repressing political demonstrations held by opposition groups, for its poor prison conditions, and for police brutality.

Although voters elected President Moi to a third term in 1988, the National Assembly was criticized for its actions that year. The assembly extended the length of time that people suspected of capital offenses could be detained without trial from twenty-four hours to fourteen days, and it voted to expand the president's power to include the right to dismiss senior judges at will.

**Amnesty International is among many nonprofit organizations that track the status of human rights in Kenya and other countries around the world. Amnesty International's mission is "preventing and ending grave abuses of the rights to physical and mental integrity, freedom of conscience and expression, and freedom from discrimination, within the context of its work to promote all human rights."**

President Moi has at times bowed to the pressure of such international criticism—and the accompanying threat of losing financial assistance. In 1989 he released all political prisoners and offered amnesty (pardon) to exiled dissidents. Also, in response to pressure, the government once again legalized a multiparty system in 1991. Later in the decade, the Moi government went on to form a human rights committee to investigate alleged abuse by authorities.

Since 1991 several bouts of ethnic conflict have occurred in the Rift Valley, Nairobi, and Mombasa. These conflicts have left 1,500 people dead and have displaced 300,000. The government has been

Safina leader **Richard E. Leakey** addresses a press conference in his Nairobi office in 1999.

accused of inciting such incidents of violence to disrupt elections and to weaken emerging political parties.

Opposition leader Oginga Odinga formed a new political party in 1991, called the Forum for the Restoration of Democracy (FORD), to challenge Moi. In that same year, former vice president Mwai Kibaki founded yet another party to challenge KANU. In August 1992, FORD split into two parties, FORD-Kenya led by Odinga, and FORD-Asili led by Kenneth Matiba.

Despite the formation of numerous political parties, none has presented a significant challenge to the dominance of the KANU party. In December 1992, in the first multiparty elections held since 1963, President Moi won a fourth five-year term. Challenges to his government's authority continued to arise, however. In 1995 the world-famous anthropologist Richard E. Leakey founded Safina, a party whose purpose was to change the existing political system. Yet another political party was founded in the mid-1990s by Raila Odinga, the son of Oginga Odinga.

In December 1997, amid allegations of election fraud and incompetence, Moi won his fifth presidential term. According to Kenya's constitution, this will be Moi's last term. New elections are scheduled for December 2002.

## Challenges Ahead

In August 1998, a car bomb exploded at the U.S. Embassy in Nairobi, killing 224 people (including 12 Americans) and injuring approximately 5,000. Simultaneously, a bomb exploded at the U.S. Embassy in Dar es Salaam, Tanzania, killing 11 and injuring 85. In response to these deadly bombings—which were suspected of being linked to al-Qaeda, an international terrorist organization headed by former Saudi Arabian citizen Osama bin Laden—the United States carried out air strikes in Afghanistan and Sudan, where al-Qaeda bases were located. In 2001 a U.S. federal court convicted four men of conspiring to and carrying out the embassy bombings. The four were later sentenced to life in prison.

Al-Qaeda and Osama bin Laden are also suspected of carrying out the 2001 terrorist attacks in New York City and Washington, D.C., that killed approximately 3,000 people and led the United States to declare a war on terrorism. Although some believe that Kenya has been used as a base for al-Qaeda and its affiliates, the government of Kenya denies this and has condemned the terrorist attacks in the United States.

Survivors help each other climb out of the wreckage following the 1998 **terrorist bombing** of the U.S. Embassy in Nairobi.

# Government

The Republic of Kenya is governed by a president and a national assembly, or parliament. All citizens over the age of eighteen are eligible to vote for the president, who is elected to a five-year term. The president appoints a vice president and cabinet ministers from the National Assembly. In 1997 membership in the National Assembly was increased from 200 to 224 members. The National Assembly consists of 210 elected members (with five-year terms), an attorney general and speaker, and 12 members appointed by the president.

The high court of Kenya has a chief justice and at least thirty judges, all of whom are appointed by the president. District courts rule on local issues.

Kenya is divided into the municipality of Nairobi and seven provinces. The provinces are further divided into fifty-three districts that administer local government. Each district has its own commissioner, who is selected by the president. Commissioners raise funds for the local concerns of their districts, such as education, public health, and transportation. Although these local political units are responsible to the national government, they exercise their duties with considerable freedom.

## CONSTITUTIONAL REFORM MOVEMENT

The constitution of Kenya was amended in 1982 to make the KANU party the only legal party, an amendment that was reversed in 1991. In 1986 the secret ballot was eliminated in primary elections, but the new system has since been abolished. In 1997 the constitution was amended once again to provide free and fair elections. At this time, detaining people without trials was also prohibited. A 1999 amendment reduced the president's control over the legislative process.

A reform movement has arisen, whose goal is to overhaul the Kenyan constitution. It argues that the current government gives too much power to the president and is unsuitable for a multiparty system. In 2001 the reform group agreed to work with an established constitutional review commission to draft a more democratic constitution.

# THE PEOPLE

Kenya is a nation of more than thirty ethnic groups with different languages and customs. One of the most difficult tasks facing the republic is achieving unity among these diverse peoples. The nation's motto, harambee—meaning "pull together"—was introduced by President Kenyatta to unite Kenyans psychologically as well as economically and politically. Of the nation's 30.3 million people, only 1 percent is non-African, including those of south Asian and European descent.

Visit vgsbooks.com for links to websites where you can tour an East African village, get additional information about the Swahili language, and learn more about Kenya's diverse peoples, including the religion and social structures of the Masai and other ethnic groups.

ethnic groups, such as the Kikuyu and the Luo, have assimilated in Kenya's African population—Bantu, Nilotic, and Cushitic. Some based on their languages. Three major language groups are represented study language) have noted similarities among these different peoples past two thousand years. Many historians and linguists (those who arisen from historical movements of peoples in East Africa during the Kenya's population. A great variety of languages and customs have

It is difficult to categorize the many ethnic groups that compose

## ◯ Ethnic Groups

large cities, English is widely used.
widely spoken. Farther north, especially around Nairobi and in other
the Arab domination of the East African coastal region, where it is still
Bantu tongue that uses many Arabic words, Swahili developed during
serves as the language of commerce among many ethnic groups. A
Swahili and English are the official languages in Kenya, and Swahili

THE PEOPLE    CULTURAL LIFE    THE ECONOMY

VGS

Western culture almost completely. Other groups, like the Masai and the Boran, have sought to retain their own traditions and cultural practices.

**BANTU-SPEAKING PEOPLES** Bantu-speakers form the largest linguistic group in Kenya, comprising about 60 percent of the population. These peoples originally inhabited three distinct regions of the country—the upper area of Lake Victoria, central Kenya, and the extreme southern portion of the coast. Although all Bantu-speaking peoples have similar customs, there are several subgroups included in this category. The largest single Bantu-speaking group in Kenya is the Kikuyu, who comprise roughly 22 percent of the population. Some of the other large Bantu-speaking groups are the Luhya, who make up 14 percent; the Kamba, who number just over 11 percent; and the Meru who make up 6 percent of the population.

**NILOTIC PEOPLES** Kenya's Nilotic peoples are named after their original location in Sudan near the Nile River. The main Nilotic group in Kenya is the Luo, the third largest ethnic group in the country—after the Kikuyu and the Luhya—making up more than 13 percent of the population. Since migrating to Kenya, the Luo have inhabited the area around Lake Victoria and its southern boundaries.

Other Nilotic peoples are concentrated in the Rift Valley of western Kenya, where the population is divided between Bantu and Nilotic groups. Like the Luo, the Nilotic people of the Rift Valley descend from groups that

originally migrated into present-day Kenya from the north. Sometimes referred to as Kalenjin, these peoples divide themselves into several smaller ethnic groups, but collectively they compose 12 percent of Kenya's population. Historically the Kalenjin have been highland farmers occupying land at elevations of between 5,000 and 8,000 feet (1,524 and 2,438 m).

The Masai, another Nilotic group, are probably the best-known ethnic group in Kenya, both because British colonists were fascinated by them and because the tourist industry highlights Masai culture. The Masai number fewer than 250,000 people, but they are well known because of their romantic reputation as fierce warriors and cattle keepers. The nomadic way of life of the Masai is dying, however, because Kenya's need to feed its growing population has reduced the land available for grazing. Without land to graze their cattle, many Masai people have settled on farms or moved to cities.

CUSHITIC PEOPLES Constituting the smallest language group in Kenya, the Cushitic peoples include those who historically inhabited northern and northeastern Kenya. Influenced by Afro-Asiatic languages spoken in northern Africa and the Arabian Peninsula, the Cushitic groups are primarily nomads who herd camels and sheep in Kenya's dry regions. The Galla and other Somali-speaking peoples, as well as the Boran—who form the largest ethnic unit in this area—are representative groups.

**Kikuyu schoolgirls** wear traditional dress to perform a Kikuyu dance. For the most part, however, the Kikuyu wear Western-style clothing.

## Education

An important aspect of life in Kenya is the government's concern for education and welfare. The largest single expense in the Kenyan annual budget goes to education. The government provides free primary schooling for eight years, although attendance is not compulsory. About 87 percent of children between the ages of six and twelve go to primary school, but only about 25 percent of children over the age of twelve attend classes. In 2000 more than three-fourths of the nation's people were literate.

In the past, elders within each ethnic community gave children a practical education. For example, children were taught ethical principles, the history of their people, and useful information for farming and raising cattle. Kenya's formal educational structure was originally modeled after the British system, with seven years of primary school and six years of secondary school. In 1985 Kenya changed its system to eight years of primary school, four years of secondary

Since English is one of the official languages in Kenya, **school libraries** are filled with books and publications familiar to English-language readers.

The **University of Nairobi** plays a prominent role in training Kenyan students for jobs in the technology marketplace.

school, and four years of university-level education. In the early 2000s, the education system was again under review, and structural change was anticipated. Experts argue that the current system does not teach the skills needed to further the country's industrial and economic development.

Students who complete the primary level must pass an examination in order to attend secondary school. (Students in secondary school must pay tuition.) After completing the four-year secondary program, students take another examination for entry into a university-level program. The Ministry of Education controls Kenya's five public universities—Egerton, Kenyatta, Moi, Nairobi, and the Kenyatta University College of Agriculture and Technology. Twelve private universities are also located in Kenya.

## ◉ Health

The government has made improved health care for Kenyans a high-priority project. Almost everywhere in the young nation, there is a growing respect for preventive medicine (practices that seek to prevent the development of health problems). Government health agencies are attempting to wipe out the conditions that cause malaria and sleeping sickness, as well as to educate Kenyans about health and sanitation.

The average life expectancy in Kenya is 49 years of age. Although this figure is slightly higher than the average of 46 for East Africa, it is well below the average of 75 for industrialized countries. Modern hospitals are located in the cities and towns, and in the rural areas there are dispensaries—which supply medical and dental care—mission hospitals, and clinics.

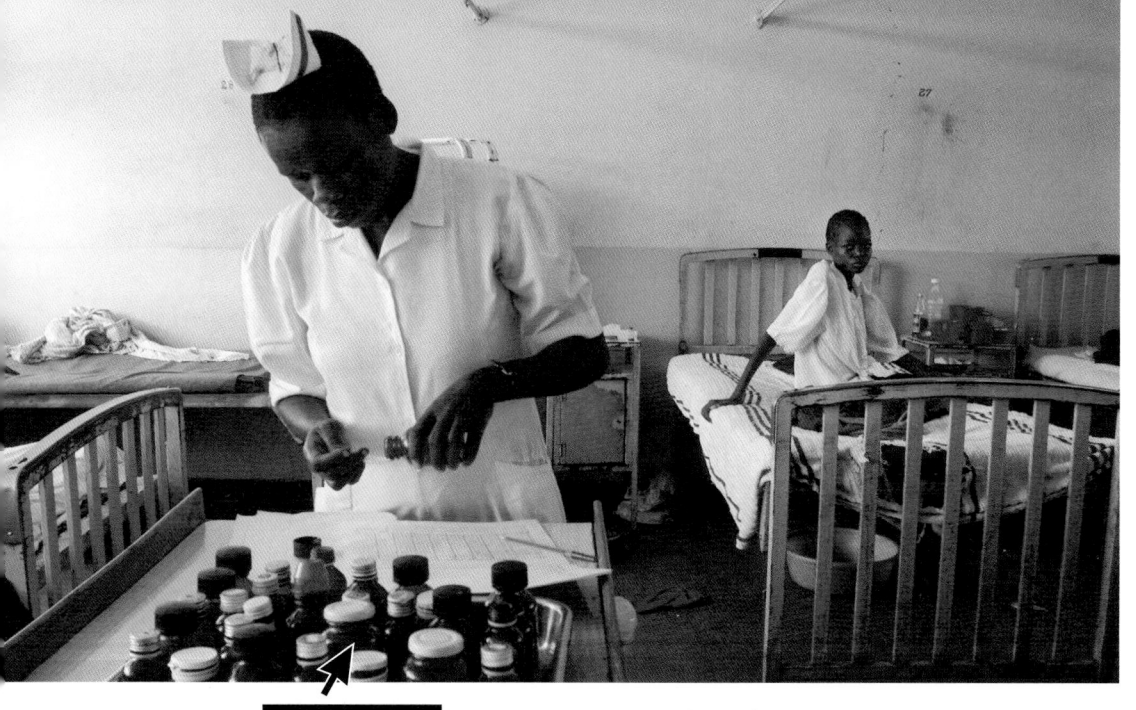

Some **health workers** in Kenya care for patients in poorly equipped clinics. The AIDS epidemic has strained Kenya's health-care system, which suffers from insufficient funding and inadequate medical expertise to deal the range of health-care issues facing the nation.

Kenya is dealing with the serious health problem of HIV (human immunodeficiency virus) and AIDS. In the late 1990s, more than 14 percent of the nation's adult population (ages fifteen to forty-nine) had HIV/AIDS, and more than 500,000 Kenyans had died of AIDS by 1999. Slightly more women than men had the disease. The consequences of this epidemic are widespread and devastating. The life expectancy rate in the country has been shortened, many children are orphaned because their parents die from AIDS, and young workers (who are most likely to contract the disease) in high-skill jobs often become sick or die. Kenya lacks adequate financial resources and the medical expertise to treat its infected people and to prevent the spread of HIV through educational and medical programs. The country relies on assistance from the international community. For its part, the Kenyan government has been slow to respond to the AIDS crisis. In 1999 President Moi announced the creation of a National AIDS Control Council to work toward control of AIDS in Kenya.

> "AIDS is not just a serious threat to our social and economic development; it is a real threat to our very existence, and every effort must be made to bring the problem under control."
> —President Daniel T. arap Moi

Another major problem facing Kenya is a 2.1 percent annual rate of population growth. This means that Kenya's current population of 30.3 million will double by the year 2034. Food requirements will also double, despite the decline in agricultural production. To lower the birthrate, international agencies have increased their contributions to family-planning programs in Kenya. However, many Kenyans refuse to participate in these programs, arguing that they conflict with their traditional values.

## SOMALI REFUGEES

The arrival of immigrants from the African country of Somalia has contributed to the surge in Kenya's population. Many of these Somali immigrants fled after civil war broke out there in the early 1990s. The Kenyan government claimed that these refugees created a burden on Kenya's resources and asked the United Nations to help. Although three-fourths of the Somali refugees had been relocated by mid-1998, more Somali refugees entered the country later in the decade, as instability continued in their homeland. In the early 2000s, Somalis made up 3 percent of Kenya's population. For a link to the most up-to-date population figures for Kenya, go to vgsbooks.com.

**Somali refugees** sit with their possessions in a refugee camp at Liboi, Kenya.

# CULTURAL LIFE

Many of Kenya's ethnic groups pride themselves on the distinct customs and ceremonies that set them apart from other groups. At the same time, some parallels can be seen in the daily life of many groups. Historically, ethnic identity has been critical in Kenya. Only in the last part of the twentieth century did marriages between ethnic groups become somewhat common. As more people move into the urban centers, however, Kenya's ethnic divisions are becoming blurred for its younger generations.

## ⊙ Customs

Most ethnic groups have common customs concerning entrance into adulthood, marriage, family life, and other practices. These customs vary in degree of ritual but not in importance. The family unit, which embraces those living together in a village—including cousins, nephews, nieces, uncles, and aunts—is extremely important.

Once children begin to earn a living, their duty is to take care of their parents. No matter where they have found employment, children will send a portion—or, in an emergency, all—of their salary home. This money may be used to help pay for educating younger children or for medical supplies for an ailing relative. Among almost all ethnic groups, the grown children take responsibility for the older people. Elderly people are treated with respect, for it is believed that the years they have lived have brought them wisdom.

## Urban and Rural Life

Although life in most Kenyan urban areas is fast paced, village life tends to follow the flow of the seasons. In the cities, many men dress in suits and ties. On festive occasions, such as Independence Day (December 12) or Kenyatta Day (October 20), many African women wear *kangas,* which are long pieces of cloth wrapped around the body. Men often wear loose-fitting, collarless dashikis (shirts) printed in bright African designs.

**Urban commuters** express their diversity in creative combinations of Western and traditional clothing.

In the country, people live a life adapted to the needs of an agricultural economy. Trips to towns are often full-day excursions by *matatu* (small bus), by taxi, by bicycle, or on foot. In October, when the harvesting is completed, the men take their farm products to the towns to sell them. They return with money or goods such as lamps, blankets, and tools.

When the farmwork is completed at the end of each day, the men usually get together to talk, either at someone's house or at *dukas* (small shops). Many parts of the country lack electricity, and the countryside is dotted with small fires during the evening hours. Whereas wealthy city dwellers can have a nightlife if they choose, rural residents usually retire early and rise early in the morning.

# ► Religion

The Kenyan government guarantees religious freedom for all its citizens, and the religious composition of the population is quite varied. Roman Catholics represent 28 percent, Protestants number 38 percent, and supporters of traditional beliefs account for 26 percent. Muslims—followers of Islam—are the smallest religious group. Comprising 6 percent of the population, they are found mostly in the coastal region. A small percentage of Hindus of East Indian ancestry worship in temples in cities and towns throughout the country.

Many of Kenya's people retain their own ethnic religious practices. Others have adopted Christianity and are church members. Many customs of the African population of Kenya have survived within the framework of the Christian churches without conflict. However, polygamy—the practice of having more than one wife—has caused some strain between the people of Kenya and the Christian churches. It has long been an African custom for a man to take as many wives as he can afford to support. In this way, the family continues to grow as the marriages produce many children who will help support the family when they are adults. Christian missionaries teach that this practice conflicts with Christian doctrine.

This **Hindu temple** in Mombasa overflows with offerings of food.

Faithful Catholics attend **Mass at a mission** on the southeastern shore of Lake Turkana.

Nevertheless, the Christian religion has played a big role in the development of Kenya, and the churches are still growing. In addition to Independence Day and Kenyatta Day, Kenya celebrates many Christian and Islamic holidays. For example, Christmas in Kenya often includes the tradition of roasting a fresh goat. Ramadan, the holiest month in the Islamic calendar, is marked by fasting from daybreak until sunset. Ramadan ends with a three-day celebration called Eid al-Fitr. Families exchange gifts and enjoy feasting to celebrate the end of the fasting period.

## Sports and Recreation

Recreational activities and sports are an important part of life in Kenya. The most popular athletic activities are soccer, track and field, cricket, and water sports. Athletes are encouraged to participate in school sports and in local and nationwide competitions. Kenyans demonstrate particular ability in distance running. Three of Kenya's best known runners are Kipchoge Keino, Olympic gold medalist in 1968 and 1972; Henry Rono, with four world athletic records in the 1970s;

Kenya captured its first Olympic medal at the 1964 Tokyo Games when Wilson Kiprugut Chuma won a bronze in the 800-meter race. Historically Kenyan athletes have brought home forty-seven Olympic medals. To learn more about Kenya's Olympic history, visit vgsbooks.com.

and Moses Kiptanui, who holds the 3000-meter world record set in 1995. Kenyan women runners who have attracted worldwide recognition include Pauline Konga, Kenya's first woman Olympic medalist at the 1996 Atlanta Games, taking the silver in the women's 5000 meters; Joyce Chepchumba, Olympic medalist in the marathon at the 2000 Sydney Games; Tegla Loroupe, who holds the world women's marathon record; and Catherine Ndereba, who won the Boston Marathon in 2000 and 2001.

Soccer is the national team sport, and Kenyan teams play many international matches with teams from Great Britain, Germany, and eastern Europe, as well as with other African nations. Schools sponsor soccer teams, and a

## IN THE LONG RUN

Kenyan distance runners have a tradition of using their prize money to help improve conditions in their communities. They start businesses with this purpose in mind. They also buy real estate. As more Kenyan women win big races like the Boston Marathon, they also become role models and benefactors.

**Catherine Ndereba** of Kenya breaks the tape to win the Women's Division of the Boston Marathon in 2000. She finished the 26-mile course in 2:26:1, or a little less than 2 1/2 hours.

nationwide league has teams representing the cities and towns of Kenya. In recent times, volleyball, hockey, boxing, karate, and tae kwon-do have also gained popularity. Nairobi has two world-class stadiums—the Moi International Sports Center and the Nyayo National Stadium.

In addition to sports, dancing has always been a popular recreational activity among Kenyans. Ethnic dances and dances introduced by Europeans are well known. For people living in cities and towns, dancing and attending movies are popular means of relaxation. In the late 1990s, Kenyans had about 730,000 televisions and 3 million radios. Five daily newspapers are published in Kenya. The Internet is relatively new in the country. About 45,000 people had Internet access in 1999.

## Literature

Kenya's literary heritage has been based on oral tradition. Myths, folktales, and proverbs have been transmitted verbally from one generation to the next and often impart a message or moral. Symbolism—the use of a tangible sign to represent something intangible, such as happiness, anger, or sadness—is an important element in this tradition. Common topics include religion, history, nature, and everyday life. Because of

Effective storytellers, such as these **Kikuyu performers** in Kenya, use every medium available—music, dance, costume, body painting, and narrative. Visit vgsbooks.com for a link where you can read a Swahili folktale in English.

the long practiced custom of storytelling, speech is considered a form of artistic expression, and those who speak well are highly respected.

The oldest form of written literature is Swahili poetry and prose from the coastal area. Prose writing was used primarily to record historical, religious, and legal matters. Initially, most poetry was recited or sung. Only later, after gaining public approval, were poems written down. Different kinds of poems follow distinct forms. For example, *mashairi* (improvised songs) traditionally have two-line stanzas, or sections, with each line containing either twelve or twenty syllables. *Tenzi* (educational poems) are composed of four-line stanzas. Tenzi, which can be more than one thousand stanzas long, are usually about subjects such as bravery, romance, history, or religion.

Recent cultural activities in Kenya have been closely connected with politics. The rise of the independence movement, for example, encouraged nationalist literature. The most famous work from this period is Jomo Kenyatta's *Facing Mount Kenya,* which descibes Kikuyu family and community life in detail.

Since independence, writers have revealed some of the inequities in their society. The contemporary works of Ngugi wa Thiong'o best illustrate this point. Ngugi's novels in the English language—*Weep Not, Child; The River Between; A Grain of Wheat;* and *Petals of Blood*—move from anticolonial themes to those of continuing economic injustice since independence. His later works in Kikuyu—a language more accessible to indigenous people—speak so directly about unfairness and government corruption that they were banned.

## ◉ Music

Music has long been a part of life in Kenya. Ethnic groups use music in their ceremonies marking the transitions of life, as well as in their daily routines. Throughout Africa, music has traditionally served as

The **eight-stringed** *nyatti* is an example of a traditional, handmade Luo instrument.

a means of expressing the experience of life, and music is incorporated into life at an early age. Children as young as three or four make musical instruments and play musical games.

Just as numerous aspects of life in Kenya have changed in the past century, so, too, has the country's music. Many worry that traditional music will disappear from Kenya, yet numerous forms of music are heard throughout the country, including hip-hop, rap, rhythm and blues, and gospel. Although much of Kenyan music was once based on European music and that of other African countries, the nation has slowly developed its own modern style of music. Benga, for example, is a popular style of contemporary dance music that originated after Kenya achieved independence. Benga uses dance rhythms that were traditionally played on the lyre. First adapted to the acoustic guitar, these rhythms are played most often on the electric guitar. Guitar music in general also continues to be a favorite in Kenya.

## Food

Traditional food in Kenya often consists of meat and beans. Most meals also include *ugali*, a maize (corn) meal, and *sukuma wiki*, a meal made from a kalelike leaf. Goat and beef are common and well liked. Chicken is served only for special occasions. Many meats are grilled. Fish, such as the Nile perch and the tilapia, are regularly eaten,

A variety of produce is available at this open-air market in Isiolo, Kenya.

## SUKUMA WIKI

This "leftovers stew" is a meat and vegetable recipe that is common in Kenya. It is served everywhere from family homes to fine restaurants.

½ pound leftover meat, cooked or raw and chopped into bite-sized pieces

1 tbsp. vegetable oil

2 onions, diced

4 tomatoes, peeled* and quartered

1 green pepper, chopped

Salt and black pepper to taste

1 pound fresh or frozen spinach, chopped

1. If you are using uncooked meat, heat the oil in a frying pan and lightly sauté the meat. When the meat is nearly cooked, add the onions and continue cooking until they are soft and translucent. Add the tomato quarters with the chopped green pepper and any other precooked meat. Season with salt and pepper to taste and cook until the meat is done.
2. Stir in the chopped spinach and cook on low heat for about 30 minutes, stirring periodically. Give the whole pan a final stir before serving.

*To peel a tomato, place it in a small saucepan of boiling water for about 1 minute. Remove with a slotted spoon and cool until the tomato is warm but no longer hot. Use a small paring knife to peel off the skin. It will come off easily.

especially in areas near Lake Victoria. Dessert is not common, but fruit is often available. Tea and beer are regularly consumed with meals.

Restaurants are becoming more popular in large cities, especially in Nairobi and Mombasa, and they feature a wide variety of foods. For example, visitors to Nairobi can choose from African, Italian, French, Japanese, Indian, Thai, vegetarian, or fast-food restaurants.

# THE ECONOMY

Under President Moi's direction, the government of Kenya has encouraged foreign investment and the development of private businesses. During the late 1990s and early 2000s, the International Monetary Fund (IMF) and the World Bank suspended and resumed aid to the country numerous times. Suspensions were due to the ongoing government corruption and to the slow progress of the privatization process. Kenya is working to strengthen the industrial and financial sectors of its economy.

The nation's debts exceed its income, and the costs of staple foods are rising. In 1997 the country had 1.2 million paid male workers and nearly 475,000 paid female workers. Yet widespread unemployment and a shortage of consumer goods create hardships for many Kenyans. Per capita gross national product (a measure of yearly earnings per person) stood at $330 in 1998—well below the average for African countries. Government corruption is a drain on the economy. The economy is also threatened by its population growth, recurrent

drought, the AIDS epidemic, and the negative impact of violence on tourism.

## ▶ Agriculture

Throughout its history, Kenya has been predominantly an agricultural nation. As a result, the national economy is subject to the uncontrollable and often unpredictable forces of the weather. Drought and floods periodically have a disastrous effect on Kenya's economy and on the standard of living for the nation's people. Although attempts have been made in recent years to introduce light industry, Kenya remains mostly a land of farmers.

Two kinds of farming are practiced extensively—subsistence farming and cash-crop farming. The difference between the two is basically economic. Subsistence farming means growing only enough crops to feed a farmer's family. Cash-crop farming means growing a certain product that is eventually sold for profit. Some farmers combine the

two types of farming, but the majority of Kenyan farmers practice subsistence farming.

Subsistence farmers in Kenya grow maize (corn), millet, rice, sweet potatoes, cassava (a fleshy root crop), bananas, potatoes, coconuts, and pineapples. Maize is probably the most widely grown crop in Kenya because it is the primary ingredient in the staple of the Kenyan diet, a stiff cornmeal dough called ugali.

The government is trying to increase cash-crop production to balance the value of its exports with the value of its imports. Government officials hope that the cultivation of cash crops will eventually replace subsistence farming. The principal cash crops for export are coffee, tea, sugarcane, maize, wheat, sisal (a fibrous plant used in rope making), pyrethrum (a natural insecticide), and cotton. Pineapples and coconuts are grown for both export and local consumption.

For many years, coffee beans were Kenya's leading export, but problems in the world markets have caused coffee prices to fall. The production of coffee has also declined in the last decade. In the mid-1990s, coffee's share in total export earnings was about 14 percent. Meanwhile, tea production has surged, reaching 267,540 tons (242,660 metric tons) in 1998 and accounting for almost 20 percent of total

With falling prices, **coffee beans** are no longer Kenya's leading export.

export earnings. Kenya's tea is of a high quality and is popular on the European market, especially in Great Britain.

Some maize is exported to other parts of East Africa, and these sales also bring cash into the country. Farmers raise cattle as a source of dairy products and meat for domestic consumption and for export. Agricultural output continues to grow. In the late 1990s, agriculture employed about 76 percent of the total labor force and made up nearly one-third of Kenya's total economy.

The leaves and daisylike flowers of the pyrethrum plant are used in making insecticides, and pyrethrum ranks high as a source of foreign income. Pyrethrum grows best in the highlands at elevations of 6,000 to 8,000 feet (1,829 to 2,438 m) above sea level. Kenya's pyrethrum farms are valuable to the country's export trade.

## Manufacturing

Kenya is one of the most industrially developed countries in East Africa. The manufacturing industry accounts for 10.5 percent of the gross domestic product and employs at least 14 percent of the workforce. Since the country achieved independence, the government has invested heavily in industrial development, and foreign countries such as the United States and Great Britain have also contributed to Kenya's

Packagers bag a gray processed powder called **kensil** at this diatomite plant in Kenya's Rift Valley. Kensil is used as an abrasive, as insulation, or as a filtering material.

industrial growth. Important industries include those that produce or process petroleum, textiles, clothing, cement, meat, food, beverages, dairy products, electrical equipment, motor vehicles, and chemicals.

## Tourism

The Kenyan government continues to view tourism as its most important source of foreign currency. Tourism rates dropped in the mid-1990s and early 2000s due to a number of factors, including conflict and crime in the country, competition from other countries in the region, and the September 11, 2001, terrorist attacks in the United States, which reduced travel around the world. Still, about one million tourists visit Kenya each year.

Traditionally, the main attraction in Kenya has been wildlife watching and photography, but beach holidays have become as popular as safari

### PLANNING A TRIP TO KENYA?

**Here are some helpful tips:**

- **The busiest months for tourism are January and February. During these months, the weather is pleasant, and the wildlife scenes are abundant.**

- **Travel to Kenya during July and August includes the treat of seeing the annual migration of wildebeests. The Masai Mara Game Reserve is the best place to see these animals.**

- **Study the health risks. Except in Nairobi, tourists may be exposed to malaria, cholera, hepatitis, meningitis, typhoid, schistosomiasis, HIV, Rift Valley fever, and yellow fever. Be sure to check with your doctor ahead of time about required and available vaccinations.**

   **For links to more information on traveling to Kenya, visit vgsbooks.com.**

A languid **lion** refuses to strike a pose.

There is plenty of fun, surf, and sun for everyone at this **Indian Ocean beach** in Mombasa.

tours. Once famous as a place for hunting game, Kenya instead encourages tourists to shoot only with cameras. In recent years, conservation of wildlife, some of whose numbers have dropped alarmingly, has become a major concern.

Of Kenya's twenty-five national parks and twenty-three reserves, some of the most famous are Nairobi, Amboseli, Meru, Tsavo, Mount Kenya, and Aberdare. Each park specializes in a particular type of wildlife, and a tourist could spend several weeks visiting all of them. For viewing elephants, Tsavo National Park is probably the best spot in Kenya. Lions are seen to best advantage in the Masai Mara Game Reserve. Other parks have a large population of wildebeests, warthogs, baboons, gazelles, impalas, and various types of birdlife. Lake Nakuru offers tourists a bird sanctuary where flamingos and ibis can be photographed.

## Transportation

With one of the best transportation systems in Africa, Kenyans depend on trains, boats, and automobiles to get around the country. Of approximately 1,700 miles (2,736 km) of track operated by the

Kenya Railways Corporation, about half of the line serves the area between Mombasa and the Ugandan border. Boats transport both goods and people along the coast and on Lake Victoria, where steamers serve the various East African lake ports, including Kisumu, Kenya's busy inland port. Kenya has about 39,330 miles (63,296 km) of roads, but only about 14 percent of them are paved.

Since achieving independence, Kenya has constructed feeder roads, which link agricultural areas to the main roads. In addition, international roads link Kenya with the neighboring countries of Somalia, Tanzania, and Ethiopia. Road transport is a popular way of moving goods in Kenya because it is faster than rail, though it may be more expensive.

Roads leading to the main highways are paved or surfaced with a loose sand and pebble mixture called *murram*. In the rainy season, these murram roads are often impassable, which delays overland transport. Since the 1980s, the condition of Kenyan roads has declined due to poor maintenance. Work to improve the condition of the major road between Nairobi and Mombasa began in the late 1990s, through a loan from the World Bank. With improved surfacing of such roads, transportation of goods and people by automobile, truck, and matatu will become less expensive, further relieving the railways of their heavy burden.

Kenya is a member of the World Bank, which offers long-term financial assistance to its member countries. One of the main goals of the World Bank is to increase the economic security of its member countries.

Kenya's government-owned airline, Kenya Airways, became partly privatized in 1996. The airline services international as well as domestic routes. Kenya has airports at Mombasa, Nairobi, Malindi, Kisumu, and Eldoret. By 2001 Kenya had three international airports—Jomo Kenyatta International Airport in Nairobi, Moi International Airport in Mombasa, and Eldoret International Airport in Eldoret.

## The Future

Kenya has been plagued by numerous setbacks—political tension and corruption, outbreaks of ethnic violence, severe drought, the AIDS epidemic, and international terrorism. Although the country is struggling to deal with these political challenges and natural disasters, life in Kenya is relatively stable, especially in comparison to conditions in many other African nations. The outcome of elections scheduled for late 2002 will reveal much about Kenya's future.

This **Airbus A310** in Kenya Airways' fleet can seat 202 passengers—18 in first class, 184 in economy.

The prosperity of Kenya in the future is also dependent on educational and health initiatives. With increased numbers of skilled professionals, the nation can improve its economy and increase its standard of living. Yet, the country must also ensure the health of its future workforce through education and healthcare programs to prevent the spread of HIV and AIDS.

As Kenya works through the complex problems of the twenty-first century, the young country can find strength by reviewing its past. For hundreds of years its people, of diverse cultural heritage, have pulled together to overcome numerous challenges.

## KENYA'S PRIVATIZATION PLAN IS LOOKING UP

Kenya's privatization plan—which is intended to strengthen the private sector's presence in the economy—is ambitious. When the plan was announced in 1991, Kenya Airways was just one of 207 government-operated businesses targeted for privatization. By 1998 the country had sold off part or all of 165 of these companies to private businesses.

**500 B.C.–A.D. 500**    Bantu-speaking and Nilotic-speaking peoples settle in Kenya.

**A.D. 500**    Inhabitants of Kenya's coast begin trading with Greeks, Romans, Persians, and East Indians.

**A.D. 900–1400**    Arab peoples dominate the coast of Kenya.

**EARLY 1400S**    Portuguese begin exploring coasts of Africa.

**1498**    Vasco da Gama leads an expedition around the southern tip of Africa and up the eastern coast toward Kenya.

**EARLY 1500S**    Portuguese win control of the Kenyan coast from the Arabs and use the area as a trading post for the next two hundred years.

**1700S**    Arabs regain control of the Kenyan/East African coast.

**1850**    European missionaries and adventurers begin exploring Kenya's interior.

**1884–1885**    At the Berlin Conference, East Africa, including present-day Kenya, is divided between Great Britain and Germany.

**1896**    British begin building the Kenya-Uganda Railroad, which eventually links Mombasa with Uganda and the Nile region.

**1905**    The British government establishes the Legislative Council.

**1914–1918**    World War I takes place.

**1920**    Great Britain officially claims Kenya as part of its empire.

**1925**    The Kikuyu Central Association (KCA), a prominent Kenyan political organization, forms, headed by Jomo Kenyatta.

**1929**    Jomo Kenyatta unsuccessfully petitions the British Parliament in person for elected black representation on the Legislative Council.

**1952–1955**    Secret political societies formed by black Kenyans, known collectively as the Mau Mau, engage in terrorist activity to challenge colonial authority. In 1952 the British colonial governor declares a state of emergency.

**1953**    All black political parties are outlawed and their leaders, including Jomo Kenyatta, are imprisoned.

**1955**    The ban on political parties is lifted—excluding the parties of the Kikuyu. Many small, ethnically based parties are formed, including the Kenya African National Union (KANU) and the Kenya African Democratic Union (KADU).

**1961**    Jomo Kenyatta is released from prison.

1963  On December 12, Kenya becomes independent from Great
      Britain. Jomo Kenyatta becomes Kenya's first prime minister.

1964  Kenya becomes a republic; Jomo Kenyatta is named the country's
      first president. Ngugi wa Thiong'o writes the prize-winning novel
      *Weep* Not, *Child.*

1978  Jomo Kenyatta dies. Vice president Daniel T. arap Moi becomes president.
      Henry Rono sets four world athletic records in track and field.

1982  The government officially declares Kenya to be a one-party state; a failed coup
      leaves hundreds dead, and the government cracks down on dissent.

1988  President Daniel T. arap Moi is elected to a third term.

1989  The international sale of ivory is banned. In response to international pressure,
      President Daniel T. arap Moi releases all political prisoners and offers a pardon to all
      exiled dissidents.

1990s Throughout the 1990s, ethnic conflicts erupt in Kenya, killing thousands and leaving tens
      of thousands homeless.

1990  Kenya's Wildlife Conservation and Management Department becomes the Kenya Wildlife
      Service (KWS) and is charged with protecting and conserving the wildlife of Kenya.

1991  The government restores a multiparty system. Former vice president Oginga Odinga forms
      a new party called the Forum for the Restoration of Democracy (FORD); former vice presi-
      dent Mwai Kibaki forms another, the Democratic Party.

1992  President Moi is elected to a fourth term in the first multiparty election since 1963.

1995  Anthropologist and conservationist Richard E. Leakey founds a political party called
      Safina.

1996  A new government human rights committee investigates alleged abuse by authori-
      ties. Pauline Konga is the first Kenyan woman to win an Olympic medal, a silver in the
      women's 5000 meters at the Atlanta Games.

1997  Amid allegations of corruption and fraud, President Moi wins his fifth term.
      Restrictions on the international ivory ban are loosened.

1998  A car bomb explodes at the U.S. Embassy in Nairobi, killing 224 and injuring 5,000.
      Kenya begins to experience a severe drought.

1999  The government creates a National AIDS Control Council.

2000  Runner Catherine Ndereba wins the Boston Marathon in 2:26:11.

2001  ACE Communications, Kenya, receives a special Emmy for distinctive
      television programming promoting the United Nations Children's Fund
      (UNICEF) "Say Yes for Children Campaign." Four men are convicted in
      a U.S. federal court of the 1998 bombing at the U.S. Embassy in
      Nairobi. Terrorist attacks on New York City and Washington,
      D.C., are linked to the 1998 bombings.

**NAME** Republic of Kenya

**AREA** 224,960 square miles (582,644 sq. km)

**MAIN LANDFORMS** Aberdare Range, Mau Escarpment, Great Rift Valley, Chalbi Desert

**HIGHEST POINT** Mount Kenya, 17,058 feet (5,199 m) above sea level

**LOWEST POINT** Sea level

**MAJOR RIVERS** Athi River, Tana River, Tsavo River, Galana River

**ANIMALS** Antelope, baboons, buffalo, cheetahs, elephants, giraffes, hartebeests, hippopotamuses, hyenas, impalas, jackals, leopards, lions, monkeys, rhinoceroses, wildebeests, zebras

**CAPITAL CITY** Nairobi

**OTHER MAJOR CITIES** Mombasa, Kisumu, Nakuru

**LANGUAGES** English (official), Swahili (national)

**MONEY UNIT** Kenya shilling. 100 cents = 1 shilling.

## KENYAN CURRENCY

In 1966, three years after gaining independence from Great Britain, Kenya adopted the Kenya shilling as its official currency. Based in part on the British-influenced East African shilling, the Kenya shilling breaks down into 100 cents. Coins come in 5-, 10-, and 50-cent pieces, as well as 1-, 5-, and 10-shilling pieces. Notes come in 50-, 100-, 200-, 500-, and 1,000-shilling amounts. In 1966 Kenya shilling notes showed the first president of the newly independent nation, Jomo Kenyatta. Later Kenya shilling notes displayed the likeness of President Daniel T. arap Moi.

Currency Fast Facts

The Kenyan flag was chosen when the country became independent from Great Britain in 1963. The flag is based on that of the Kenya African National Union and includes the political party's colors. Black represents the people. Red represents the struggle for freedom. Green represents the country's natural resources. The two intervening white stripes represent peace and unity. The striped flag is further decorated with a shield and spears. These represent Kenya's pride, tradition, and defense of freedom.

Adopted in 1963, the Kenyan national anthem lyrics are credited to a group of citizens. The music is a traditional melody. Following are the first two stanzas of the English version of the anthem:

O God of all creation
Bless this our land and nation
Justice be our shield and defender
May we dwell in unity
Peace and liberty
Plenty be found within our borders.

Let one and all arise
With hearts both strong and true
Service be our earnest endeavour
And our homeland of Kenya
Heritage of splendour
Firm may we stand to defend.

Want to listen to Kenya's national anthem? Go to vgsbooks.com.

**JOYCE CHEPCHUMBA** (b. 1970) Chepchumba, a long-distance runner born in Kericho, won an Olympic bronze medal in the marathon at the 2000 Summer Games in Sydney, Australia. She also won the LaSalle Bank Chicago Marathon in 1998 and 1999 and the London Marathon in 1997 and 1999. Chepchumba has broken the mold of women athletes in Kenya, as she continues to compete even though she is married and has one son.

**KIPCHOGE KEINO** (b. 1940) Born in Kipsano, Keino is considered by some to be Africa's greatest athlete. In 1965 he broke the world record for both the 3000-meter and 5000-meter races. He also possesses two gold and two silver medals from the 1968 and 1972 Olympics. He went on to coach Kenya's Olympic runners from 1976 to 1986 and to serve on the National Olympic Committee of Kenya in the 1990s. In 2000 he became a member of the International Olympic Committee. Keino and his wife have housed more than one hundred orphaned children over a thirty-year span.

**JOMO KENYATTA** (1893–1978) After years of struggling to free Kenya from British control, Jomo Kenyatta became Kenya's first president in 1964. Before that time, this Kikuyu man born in Ng'enda led the Kenya African Union and was imprisoned from 1953 until 1961 for his part in the nationalist movement known as the Mau Mau uprising. Upon his release, he worked with the British to negotiate Kenya's new constitution and to achieve Kenya's independence in 1963. In his role as Kenya's first president, Kenyatta worked to unite the numerous ethnic groups of Kenya, to establish national pride, to replace the colonial economic and cultural systems, and to expand education. He wrote *Facing Mount Kenya* and *Suffering without Bitterness*.

**RICHARD E. LEAKEY** (b. 1944) The second son of Louis and Mary Leakey, world-renowned anthropologists, Richard naturally became interested in the study of human evolution. Leakey, born in Kabete, has had a variety of careers, working as an anthropologist, a museum administrator, a conservationist, and a politician. In 1995 he founded the political party Safina. He has served as a member of parliament, as head of the National Museums of Kenya, as director of the Kenya Wildlife Service, as head of the Civil Service, and as Secretary to the Kenyan Cabinet, a position from which he resigned in 2001.

**TEGLA LOROUPE** (b. 1973) Born in the Rift Valley, Loroupe holds the world record in the women's marathon at 2:20:43. Her wins include the New York City Marathon in 1994 and 1995, the Rotterdam Marathon in the Netherlands in 1998, and the Berlin Marathon in 1999.

**WANGARI MAATHAI** (b. 1940) Maathai is the Kenyan teacher, born in Nyeri, who founded the Green Belt movement—a tree-planting project to

combat soil erosion, to slow the spread of the desert, and to provide scarce firewood to families. Since the movement began, more than 500,000 Kenyans—mostly women farmers—have planted millions of trees.

**MARJORIE OLUDHE MACGOYE** (b. 1928) MacGoye was born in Southampton, England, and came to Kenya in 1954 as an Anglican missionary. She is one of the most widely known and respected writers in contemporary Kenya. Her works include *Present Moment, Homing In* and *Chira*, as well as poetry, nonfiction, and children's books.

**ANN MCCREATH** (b. 1962) Born in Dumfries, Scotland, McCreath founded Kiko Romeo—the leading haute couture fashion house in Nairobi—to promote original, Kenya-made African fashions internationally. As head designer, she won second prize in the 1998 Smirnoff Fashion Awards and served as a judge for that competition in 2000.

**DANIEL T. ARAP MOI** (b. 1924) Moi was born in Baringo District. He began serving as vice president under Jomo Kenyatta in 1967 and became president when Kenyatta died in 1978. He was reelected to his fifth term in 1997. Although popular when he first took office, his popularity has waned with continual allegations of corruption and human rights violations.

**OGINGA ODINGA** (1911–1994) A member of the Luo ethnic group born in Siaya District, Odinga was elected to the Legislative Council in 1957. In 1960 he was named vice president of the Kenya African National Union. He served as vice president under Jomo Kenyatta from 1964 to 1966, when he left the post to form an opposition party, the Kenya People's Union (KPU). He continually criticized the government for corruption and human rights violations, and he worked to promote a multiparty system. He formed a new political party in 1991 called the Forum for the Restoration of Democracy (FORD), and made an unsuccessful bid for the presidency.

**HENRY RONO** (b. 1952) Within a three-month period in 1978, Henry Rono became the first athlete in history to set four world athletic records (in the 5,000-meter race; in the 3,000-meter steeplechase; and in 10,000-meter, and 3,000-meter races).

**NGUGI WA THIONG'O** (b. 1938) Ngugi wa Thiong'o was born in Kamiriithu. Considered Kenya's leading novelist, he wrote the prize-winning *Weep Not, Child* in 1964—the story of a Kikuyu family during the Mau Mau uprising of the 1950s. His other titles in English include *Decolonising the Mind, The River Between,* and *Petals of Blood.* In 1986 he began writing only in the Bantu language of Kikuyu or in Swahili to promote African-language literature. He has been living in exile since 1982 and joined the faculty of New York University in 1993.

**AMBOSELI NATIONAL PARK** In view of Africa's highest mountain, Mount Kilimanjaro (in Tanzania), this national park offers viewing of more than fifty species of large mammals and four hundred bird species. Amboseli National Park was the setting of literary works on big-game hunting by Ernest Hemingway and Robert Ruark. The park is the home of the Masai people.

**FORT JESUS** Dating back to 1593, this Portuguese fort in Mombasa has been turned into a museum that features displays on the Portuguese, Italian, and Arab-Islamic influences on the region.

**GEDE** The city of Gede, located 10 miles (16 km) south of Malindi, vanished in the 1600s. Partially excavated and restored, the site reveals much about the city's past inhabitants.

**LAKE VICTORIA** In area, the world's second largest freshwater lake, Lake Victoria is the headwaters of the Nile River. Tourists can enjoy a day of fishing, birdwatching, or feasting on local fish.

**LAMU** Life in this remote island city carries on much as it has for centuries. Donkeys and dhows (Arab sailing boats) are the only forms of transportation in Lamu. The city also offers spectacular Islamic architecture, beautiful beaches, and a waterfront museum.

**MASAI MARA GAME RESERVE** The rolling hills of this reserve, dubbed Kenya's "finest wildlife sanctuary," provide ample views of lions, elephants, rhinoceroses, gazelles, cheetahs, and leopards. A spectacular event is the annual march of the wildebeest, which occurs in late June as the animals trek 500 miles (800 km) across the Serengeti Plain in Tanzania back to the Masai Mara.

**MOMBASA** Built on an island, the port city of Mombasa began as an Arab center and is still influenced by that culture. Visitors can stroll the shop-lined streets to buy spices, antiques, and African crafts.

**MOUNT KENYA** The country's highest mountain at 17,058 feet (5,199 m), Mount Kenya is home to a national park where visitors can enjoy a day of walking and hiking. Below the park lies a forest rich in wildlife, including elephants, buffalo, antelope, and lions. Serious climbers enjoy the challenge of scaling Mount Kenya.

**NAIROBI NATIONAL MUSEUM** An archaeological wonderland, this museum displays scenes from the early history of human life, ceremonial dress of various ethnic groups, crafts, paintings, and an exhibit illustrating Kenya's road to independence.

**WATAMU** Tourists to Kenya come for more than the wildlife—they come for the beaches too. Watamu combines the two, with a spectacular coral reef at its marine park and beaches nestled between rocky outcrops.

**amnesty:** forgiveness or freedom granted by a government or other authority for a group of people from the penalties they would otherwise endure for their actions or offenses

**benga:** a popular style of dance music in Kenya. Often associated with the Luo people, benga began in the 1960s and gained popularity throughout much of Kenya during the 1970s.

**cash-crop farming:** a type of farming in which some of the food grown is intended to be sold for profit

**colony:** a settlement in which the residents remain tied politically and economically to another country, often called a parent country. The residents of a colony are called colonists.

**coup:** a quick and violent overthrow of government leaders, usually by a small group of people who disagree with them

**drought:** a period, usually several months long, when a region receives no precipitation or significantly less than normal. Droughts can have devastating effects on farming and water and power supplies.

**human rights:** the rights to which all humans are entitled at birth. They are generally regarded as including the right to be free from torture, execution, and unlawful imprisonment.

**Mau Mau:** a secret society of black Kenyans who, in the 1950s, used acts of violence against white Europeans and the colonial government to prevent independence from Great Britain without assuring political equality for black Kenyans

**nationalism:** a feeling of loyalty or patriotism toward one's nation, with a primary emphasis on the promotion of a national culture and national interests

**poaching:** illegal hunting. Poachers in Kenya often hunt elephants and rhinoceroses for their ivory tusks and horns.

**protectorate:** a country that is under the control, or authority, of another country (called the protector)

**republic:** a country ruled by the people, usually under the leadership of a president and other elected officials

**safari:** The word *safari* is of Arabic origin and refers to a journey. Safaris are traditionally thought of as exotic adventures or hunting expeditions to the wilderness areas of eastern Africa.

**subsistence farming:** a type of farming in which all of the food grown is intended to feed only one's family

**Swahili:** a Bantu language spoken in much of East Africa, including Kenya.

***BBC (British Broadcasting Corporation) News Online.***
**Website:** <http://news.bbc.co.uk/low/english/world/africa/default.stm/>
This is a good site to learn more about ongoing events in Africa.

**Central Intelligence Agency (CIA), *The World Factbook.***
**Website:** <http://www.odci.gov/cia/publications/factbook/index.html>
*The World Factbook* contains basic information on a country's geography, people, economy, government, communications, transportation, military, and transnational issues.

***CNN.com.***
**Website:** <http://www.cnn.com>
This is an excellent site for up-to-date articles about current events in Kenya and around the world.

***The East African Weekly.***
**Website:** <http://www.nationaudio.com/News/EastAfrican/current/index.htm>
On this site, users can find articles about recent happenings in East Africa, including regional news, business and sports news, and opinion pieces.

***The Europa World Year Book 2000.* London: Europa Publications Limited, 2000.**
This annual publication includes statistics on everything from agriculture and tourism to education and population density. It also contains a long, detailed account of Kenya's history, current events, government, military, economy, social welfare, education, and a list of public holidays. Another survey explains details of Kenya's government structure, function, and constitution.

***Lonely Planet World Guide.***
**Website:** <http://www.lonelyplanet.com/destinations/africa/kenya/>
This guide contains information for travelers to Kenya, including a list of attractions and events, currency facts and traveling costs, and a brief lesson in Kenyan culture.

***Population Reference Bureau.***
**Website:** <http://www.prb.org/>
The annual statistics on this site provide a wealth of data on Kenya's population, birth and death rates, fertility rate, infant mortality rate, and other useful demographic information.

***Statistical Abstract of the World.* Detroit: Gale Research, 1997.**
This is the source to turn to for economic and social data worldwide. You'll also find a comprehensive directory of each country's government, diplomatic representation, press, and trade organizations.

**Turner, Barry, ed. *The Statesman's Yearbook: The Politics, Cultures, and Economics of the World, 2001.* New York: Macmillan Press, 2000.**
This source clearly and succinctly presents statistical information as well as the latest details about a country's educational system, administration, defense, and energy and natural resources.

### United Nations Statistics Division.
**Website:** <http://www.un.org/Depts/unsd/>
This UN site provides a wide range of statistics, including economic, environmental, social, and demographic data.

### Washingtonpost.com.
**Website:** <http://www.washingtonpost.com/>
With its archives extending back to 1977, the *Washington Post* online is an excellent source for in-depth articles on Kenya's recent history. A small fee is charged for downloading full stories in the archives.

### Africa in Books, Music, and Videos

Website: <http://www.jambokenya.com/books/index.html>

If you want to find out more about Kenya, check out this site, called *Kenya Kitabu*. It is a source for books, music, and videos about Kenya and East Africa, on subjects ranging from biking and hiking safaris to studies on Kenyan culture.

### Crowther, Geoff, and Hugh Finlay. *Lonely Planet East Africa.* Oakland, CA: Lonely Planet, 1997.

This guide contains practical information for travelers to Kenya, including a section on Swahili, a color guide to the country's magnificent wildlife, and more than one hundred maps.

### Dinesen, Isak. *Out of Africa.* New York: Modern Library, 1992.

This well-known novel, also a movie, was first published in 1937. Written by Danish author Karen Blixen under a pen name, the stories here come from the twenty years that Blixen spent as the owner of a coffee plantation in East Africa. The book vividly describes the people, land, and wildlife of Kenya.

### Embassy of the Republic of Kenya
### 2249 R Street, NW
### Washington, D.C. 20008

Website: <http://www.kenyaembassy.com/>

Learn about the history, economy, culture, and government of Kenya straight from the country's embassy. The embassy's website also contains information about visiting Kenya and features colorful photos.

### *Expression Today* (November, 2000)

Website: <http://www.kenyanews.com>

This Kenyan journal offers political articles and opinion pieces regarding human rights, democracy, and the media in Kenya.

### Kingdon, Jonathon. *The Kingdon Field Guide to African Mammals.* San Diego, CA: Academic Press, 1997.

This guide to one thousand mammals in Africa includes identification, classification, and species information. It includes 480 color illustrations and 280 maps.

### MacGoye, Marjorie Oludhe. *Present Moment.* New York: Feminist Press, 2000.

Set in Nairobi, this African novel tells the story of seven Kenyan women over a sixty-year period. The stories, written by a contemporary Kenyan author, provide readers with a sense of Kenya's history as it affected women from diverse backgrounds.

### Pringle, Laurence. *Elephant Woman: Cynthia Moss Explores the World of Elephants.* New York: Atheneum, 1997.

Appropriate for readers ages nine through twelve, this book explains how photodocumentarian Cynthia Moss began studying elephants at a national park in Kenya. It also describes how elephants interact within their families.

**Tiffen, Mary, Michael Mortimore, and Francis Gichuki.** *More People, Less Erosion: Environmental Recovery in Kenya.* **New York: John Wiley and Sons, 1994.**

Looking at the Machakos District of Kenya—an area transformed from eroding hillsides into productive farmed terraces—this study explores how population growth in low-density areas can affect economic and social development, technological growth, and the environment.

**Trillo, Richard.** *Kenya: Rough Guide.* **New York: Rough Guides, 1997.**

This well written travel guide is popular even among Nairobi locals. It includes details on all of the most popular tourist sites in Kenya, plus information on the local art scene, restaurants, hotels, and campsites. The book also contains seventy-five maps.

*vgsbooks.com*

**Website: <http://www.vgsbooks.com>**

Visit vgsbooks.com, the homepage of the Visual Geography Series®. You can get linked to all sorts of useful on-line information, including geographical, historical, demographic, cultural, and economic websites. The vgsbooks.com site is a great resource for late-breaking news and statistics.

**Western, David.** *In the Dust of Kilimanjaro.* **Washington, D.C.: Island Press, 1997.**

David Western has penned an autobiography of his struggle to protect the wildlife of Africa. Yet, this book is more than the story of one man. It also explores the greater subjects of preserving species and protecting ecosystems.

**Wilkes, Sybella.** *One Day We Had to Run: Refugee Children Tell Their Stories in Words and Paintings.* **Brookfield, CT: Millbrook Press, 1995.**

The stories in this children's book, for ages nine through twelve, follow three children who fled to Kenya from their homes in Somalia, Sudan, and Ethiopia. The book includes color and black-and-white photographs.

**Zimmerman, Dale A., Donald A. Turner, David J. Pearson, and Ian Willis.** *Birds of Kenya and Northern Tanzania.* **Princeton, NJ: Princeton University Press, 1996.**

Bird enthusiasts can turn to this guide to learn about the 1,100 species in Eastern Africa. The book includes information on each bird's appearance, plumage, vocalization, habits, status, and distribution.

**Captions for photos appearing on cover and chapter openers:**

Cover: Wildlife photographers enjoy a hot air balloon safari in Kenya. Zebras graze undisturbed.

pp. 4–5 Animals roaming a wildlife preserve outside of Nairobi take the city's growth in stride.

pp. 8–9 The Masai Mara Game Reserve encompasses 646 square miles (1,672 sq. km) of African grasslands.

pp. 40–41 Going to the market, such as this one in Karatina, is a social event as well as an economic necessity.

pp. 48–49 Drummers perform in traditional clothing at a resort near Mount Kenya.

pp. 58–59 A sweeping view of fertile farms in the Great Rift Valley.

**Photo Acknowledgments**
The photographs in this book are reproduced with the permission of: © Mark and Denny Seaburg, pp. 4-5; © Reuters NewMedia Inc./CORBIS, pp. 7, 38, 53, and 65; © Michele Burgess, pp. 8-9, 13-14, 15, 17, 40-41, 42-43, 44, 48-49, 54, 58-59, and 68; © Nancy Smetstad-Koons, pp. 10-11; © TRIP/D. Saunders, pp. 16-17, 51, 62; © TRIP/R Daniell, pp. 18, 26, and 60; © TRIP/W. Jacobs, p. 20; © TRIP/E. Webb, p. 21; © Bettmann/CORBIS, pp. 24, 32-33, and 34; © Jeffrey L. Rotman/CORBIS, pp. 27, and 52; © Hulton-Deutsch Collection/CORBIS, pp. 29, and 30-31; © Hulton /Archive, p. 35; © AFP/CORBIS, pp. 37, and 46; © TRIP/N. Price, p. 45; © Carmen Redondo/CORBIS, p. 47; © David & Peter Turnley/CORBIS, p. 50; © TRIP/H. Luther, p. 55; © TRIP/L. Reemer, p. 56; © Ecoscene/CORBIS, p. 61; ©TRIP/Ken Powell, p. 63.

Cover photo: © TRIP/D. Saunders. Back cover photo: NASA.